Ruby the Service Dog

By Lilly Brown

ISBN:
978-1-365-78006-6

Table of Contents

"To Keely, with Love"
—L.B.

Chapter 1
On the Phone

"Hi!" said Liz. She was on the phone with her friend Mandy.

"Oh, hi, Liz did you hear the news?" asked Mandy excitedly.

"Yes! You are getting a service dog," said Liz.

"Yeah! How did you know?" inquired Mandy.

"Well, your mom told my mom then my mom told me and then I told everyone that I know in school!" said Liz.

"Thank you so much, Liz!" exclaimed Mandy. "And when we hang out, we will play fetch, Frisbee, tug-of-war and much, much more with the dog!"

"Yeah? Get this!" shouted Liz.

"What?" asked Mandy.

"You now have $8,000!" shouted Liz. "Because everyone that I told at school donated $1,000 and I donated $1,000!"

“Wow, I don’t know what to say,” said Mandy.

“You don’t have to ‘cause they are already training her,” said Liz. “You will be able to get your dog soon enough!”

“OMG, thanks,” said Mandy.

“Let’s go out to celebrate and have some burritos at ChipolteTaco.” Mandy and Liz said at the exact same time.

Chapter 2

At ChipolteTaco

When they got to ChipolteTaco, they saw a sign that read:

"Thou must be doth 16 years or older to come in by thyself!!"

"Good," said Liz. "I'm 17 and you are 16!"

"We can go in without our lazy parents!" finished Mandy.

"Yeah, like we like won't like need like our

like lazy like parents!" Liz joked.

The two girls burst out laughing!

On the door there was a blue button that had a handicapped symbol on it.

"Once I get my dog," Mandy thought. "She'll be able to press that button and open the door for me."

*　　　　　　　　*　　　　　　　　*

Once they got to their table, Mandy saw a service dog. It was from the exact same place as she was getting her dog.

Mandy got up and walked over to the table where the dog was and asked the owner, “Hey, what is your dog’s name?”

“Ruby. I am training her for a girl named Mandy. Do you know Mandy?” The trainer asked.

“Why I *am* Mandy!” Answered Mandy. “Is it a girl or a boy?”

“It's a girl!” said the trainer. “And tomorrow is your mom’s last night over at the training center. She is then going to go home and get you. Then you will do the same thing as she did," said the trainer.

"Man," Mandy said. "I had no idea all of this was goin' on!"

The trainer got up to leave.

"Wait! One more question," said Mandy.

"What?" asked the trainer.

"What's your name?" asked Mandy.

"Oh, well my name's Aryn," said the trainer. "Bye! See you soon!"

The trainer left. As Mandy saw Ruby walk across the floor of ChipolteTaco, she knew that the dog she had just met was gonna be a perfect fit for her.

Chapter 3
Aryn

"Honey, let's get going," said Mandy's Mom, Alice.

"Coming!" said Mandy

"Ready?" Asked Alice after Mandy had finished getting on her shoes and coat.

"Yep," said Mandy.

"Let's hit the road!" said Alice.

* * *

It was a 15 minute drive to the training center.

When they got there, they saw Aryn waving at them.

"Hi, again!" Aryn said to Mandy and her Mom.

"How old are you, Mandy?" Aryn asked after Mandy and her Mom were out of the car and were walking toward the main building. Mandy thought that the building looked more like a modest house, rather than a service dog headquarters.

"17," said Mandy. "Just turned it today!"

"Congratulatios! I loved being 17. And what school do you go to?" Asked Aryn.

"I go to a private school named Dog High School."

"Do you have nice or mean teachers?" Asked the trainer.

"I have…nice teachers…I guess," said Mandy.

"Alright!" said Aryn. "Let's start training Ruby!"

Chapter 4

The Training

Mandy trained for six hours and was having sooooo much fun, so she lost track of time. Alice tried to get Mandy's attention, and finally she did.

"Time to go to the house where we are going to sleep," said Alice.

"Alright, alright, can I bring Ruby with us?" asked Mandy.

"Why of course you can!" Aryn said.

"Great! Can I hold the leash?" asked Mandy.

"Why of course you can! She is your dog after all!" answered Aryn.

"Ruby, lets go!" said Mandy.

* * *

On the way to the house, Mandy quizzed herself on the commands and quizzed Ruby on *her* commands like: "wait," "left," "right" "sit," "stay," "come," and "down."

By the time Mandy said "down" for the 17th time, they were outside their dorm.

Chapter 5

1st Overnight

"Wow!" said Mandy. "I always wanted a bunk bed!"

"Woof, woof," barked Ruby.

"Time to feed Ruby," said Aryn when they got inside the house.

"Where, and how do I feed her?" asked Mandy.

"Over there," said Aryn. "Use the brown dog food and pour a half a cup into the bowl that is labeled, "Ruby.""

"Lets go!" Mandy commanded Ruby.

While Mandy fed Ruby, her mom asked Aryn some questions.

After a few seconds, Ruby came trotting out of the room and Mandy followed her.

"Now, time for *us* to eat dinner," said Aryn.

"Ruby, down," commanded Mandy. Ruby went down.

Mandy, Alice, and Aryn all ate mac and cheese for dinner. It was the best dinner of Mandy's life.

"You will have to take Ruby out for walks before and after each meal and in between,"Aryn informed Mandy. "And, Mandy you have to get up super early in the morning."

"What time?" asked Mandy.

"Oh, at 6:00 in the morning." said Aryn.

"Whew, that's *early!*" exclaimed Mandy.

"And, you, Alice have to go on 1 or 2

walks with Mandy and Ruby until Mandy gets used to her service animal."

"But I am *already* used to Ruby," said Mandy.

"Either way," said Aryn. "Oh, here, this is the afternoon schedule for you until you get used to the routine.

5:00 p.m.	Ruby's Dinner

5:30p.m.	*Your* Dinner
9:00p.m.	Night Walk

"Now let us get some shuteye!" Aryn said.

Aryn walked to her room and Mandy's Mom went right to sleep. What about Mandy? She was up late at night reading to Ruby.

Chapter 6
The 2nd Day

“Good morning Mandy!” said Aryn.

“Good morning everyone” said Mandy.

“Here is the morning schedule,” said Aryn handing Mandy the schedule.

6:20 a.m.	Morning Walk

6:30 a.m.	Ruby's Breakfast Time/Mandy's Breakfast
6:33 a.m.	Play with Ruby
6:36 a.m.	Start Working
4:45 p.m.	End Working.

"I get to do this?" asked Mandy.

"Yup," said Aryn.

"AWSOME!" exclaimed Mandy.

"Today, after training, you'll be able to bring Ruby home with you!" said Aryn.

"YES!!" Said Mandy. "Let's get training.

"The sooner the better," said Aryn.

"OK, I'll get Ruby," said Mandy.

"Let's go!!!" said Alice.

"I'll do so good in training today," said Mandy.

"Great! Let's get going to the training place!" said Aryn.

“Let’s go!” Mandy commanded Ruby.

Chapter 7
HOME!!

After 5 hours of training, they finally finished.

"Mandy?" asked Aryn.

"Yeah?" said Mandy.

"I think you and Ruby are ready to go home!" said the Aryn.

"Ruby, did you hear that?" asked Mandy

"Woof! Woof!" said Ruby

"Yes Mandy," said Alice. "You get to take her home!"

"Mom, can we show Ruby the car?" asked Mandy.

"Why, of course!" said Alice.

"Ruby, want to see our car?" asked Mandy. "It's really neat."

"Woof! Woof! Woof!" said Ruby

"She said 'yes please, Mandy' " said Alice.

"Let's show her!" said Mandy.

"OK," said Alice.

"Lets go!" Mandy commanded.

Sniff, sniff. Ruby smelled the car.

"Time to go, Mandy!" said Alice.

"You ready, you ready, UP!" Mandy commanded Ruby. Ruby jumped right into the car and plopped down on Mandy's seat.

Mandy and her Mom got into the car. Her Mom revved up the engine.

"By Aryn!" Mandy said.

"By Mandy and Ruby!" Aryn replied.

Alice steered the car out of the parking lot.

On the way home, Ruby licked Mandy's face the whole 15 minutes.

The End

About the Author and her dog.

Lilly Brown is an author, an actor and a horseback rider who has won several medals. She resides in Concord, Massachusetts with her service dog, Keely Brown.

Notes:

Notes:

www.ingramcontent.com/pod-product-compliance
Ingram Content Group UK Ltd.
Pitfield, Milton Keynes, MK11 3LW, UK
UKHW041901190726
13854UKWH00003B/1021